P9-CBM-009

i miss you!

i miss you!

a military kid's book about deployment

Beth Andrews, LCSW

Illustrated by
Hawley Wright

 Prometheus Books

59 John Glenn Drive
Amherst, New York 14228-2197

Published 2007 by Prometheus Books

Inquiries should be addressed to

Prometheus Books

59 John Glenn Drive

Amherst, New York 14228–2197

VOICE: 716–691–0133, ext. 207

FAX: 716–564–2711

WWW.PROMETHEUSBOOKS.COM

11 10 09 08 07   5 4 3 2 1

Library of Congress Cataloging-in-Publication Data

Andrews, Beth.
    I miss you! : a military kid's book about deployment / by Beth Andrews.
       p. cm.
    Includes bibliographical references.
    ISBN 978–1–59102–534–4 (alk. paper)
    1. Children of military personnel—United States—Juvenile literature. 2. Families of military personnel—United States—Juvenile literature. 3. Separation (Psychology) in children—Juvenile literature. I. Title. II. Title: Military kid's book about deployment.
U766.A47 2007   *2721*
362.82'9—dc22

2007001614

Printed in the United States of America on acid-free paper

CONTENTS

This book is dedicated to my
favorite military kids,

Shannon and Patrick

ACKNOWLEDGMENTS

Thanks to the following for their ideas on staying close with a deployed parent (pages 44 to 53):

Angela Sweeten

Leigh Macias

Marine Corps Family Network (www.marinefamily.com)

Military Advantage, Inc. (www.military.com)

GUIDE FOR FAMILY MEMBERS AND OTHER CARING ADULTS

Military families face stressful times that are unique to the military lifestyle.

Deployment is one of the most difficult situations, both for children and for parents. It is difficult for the person who is gone because he is often exhausted, living in poor conditions, lonely, feeling helpless to solve problems at home, and missing his family terribly.

Deployment is difficult for the children because they miss their parent and feel sad, angry, afraid, anxious, and lonely. Because children do not know how to express or understand these feelings, they often act them out in their behavior. Younger children may not understand why their parent is gone, only that Mom or Dad has disappeared. Since they do not have the concepts of time or perspective that adults have, it feels like forever to them.

For older children there is more of an understanding intellectually, but they may also have more worries about their parent's safety. Some of the same feelings may be present if it is another family member who the child is close to.

Deployment is difficult for the caregivers who are left behind because they often get the brunt of the children's anger, sadness, despair, and fear and don't know how to help them feel better. This all comes at a time when they are feeling great sadness, fear, and loneliness themselves. Added to this is the stress of the responsibility of making decisions, coping with crises, and handling a household and children alone. They may be at their worst and most stressed out just when the children are at their worst—withdrawn, whiny, throwing tantrums, needy, clingy, oppositional, or angry.

How This Book Can Help

The purpose of this book is to help children:

1. Understand what deployment is and why their parent has to leave.

2. Identify and understand their feelings and reactions.

3. Cope with their feelings in a positive way.

4. Know that they are not alone.

5. Try new things to help themselves feel better.

This book should be read by or to children with the help of a parent or other caring adult and then used for further discussion. It does not necessarily have to be completed all at once. Read one section at a time, stopping to discuss it before moving on.

This book encourages children to draw their feelings and experiences because drawing pictures seems to help children cope with feelings, especially for young children who don't yet know the words to use to describe what they think or feel. Talk about the drawings and your child's feelings and thoughts as much as your child wants.

Stages of Deployment

Pincus et al. (2001) identified five separate emotional stages that families go through in deployment, and the feelings and difficulties that go with each:

Predeployment starts with the warning order for deployment and ends when the parent actually leaves. Typically, families go back and forth between denial and anticipation of loss, which results in a sort of psychological pulling away. It is common for spouses to have a major argument as a way of buffering the pain of the loss. Children may cry, throw tantrums, regress, or withdraw.

Deployment is the period from the parent's departure through the first month of deployment. Here there can be a great deal of sadness, numbness, worry, and loneliness for everyone. Families may feel overwhelmed and disoriented.

Sustainment is the bulk of the separation. Spouses may begin to feel more confident as they find new support systems and develop a routine. Reactions in children often depend on the age of the child. Infants and toddlers usually do well if their parent/caregiver is doing well and does not become too depressed. Preschoolers may regress, become more cranky, or become more clingy. School-age children may whine and complain more, begin acting out their feelings in their behavior, or they may withdraw. Adolescents may become more rebellious, irritable, may fight, or do other behaviors to get attention.

Redeployment is defined as the month before the parent comes home. There is often a mix of excitement and anxiety about the reunion.

Postdeployment happens after the homecoming and is often, surprisingly, the most difficult. After a "honeymoon" period, children may react in different ways depending on their age and level of understanding. Infants and toddlers are often slow to warm up and sometimes do not recognize their parent. Older children may be very clingy or feel scared and guilty. Teenagers may be moody and distant. Children of all ages may be angry that their parent has been gone. Some children show anxiety for as long as a year after the homecoming out of fear that the parent will leave again.

Helping Your Child Cope with Deployment

Sitting down with your child and this book is a good way to begin. Here are some ongoing ways you can help your child cope:

1. When possible, talk as a family before the deployment happens. With older children, give as much advance warning as possible to give them time to adjust to the idea. With younger children, a few days to a week are probably better. Encourage them to express feelings and ask questions, and respond using "honesty with restraint." This means answering a child's questions honestly, but not giving them more information than they need. Fit the answers to their age and developmental level.

Military Advantage, Inc., an informational Web site for military families, suggests that you do not lie and do not make promises that you may not be able to keep, but do not give kids a lot of anxiety-provoking details. It is also OK to say "I don't know."

2. It is important for children to hear that their parents love them and that it is not their fault that a parent has to go away. It is also important for the parent who is going away to say good-bye, and not just disappear during the night.

3. Tell relatives, friends, teachers, daycare providers, coaches, chaplains, and others so they can give your child extra support and attention during this time. If your child is in a school with other military kids, that can be a good support. Don't be afraid to ask for help, especially when you are feeling overwhelmed.

4. Listen to your child and help him or her identify and name feelings. Respond in a nonjudgmental way, and communicate your acceptance of whatever feelings are there. Teach them positive ways to express their feelings (see pages 30–31 and 38–41).

5. Limit the amount of news, especially television. This is especially important during wartime. Younger children can be traumatized by the graphic images on TV, so save it for after they are in bed. With older children, watch the news with them and discuss it afterward (Macias; Sweeten).

6. Children should not be expected to take over adult responsibilities around the house. It is also important not to burden children with your worries or expect them to listen to your problems. Find other caring adults who you can talk to, such as friends, neighbors, relatives, support groups, clergy, and therapists.

7. Be consistent with rules, discipline, and routine. This gives children a sense of safety and security (Macias).

8. Children are very good at sensing your feelings. If you are doing well, they will cope better. Take care of yourself. Don't use alcohol and drugs to cope. Exercise, eat a healthy diet, and get enough sleep.

   Take breaks to do activities you enjoy and to be with other adults. Remember, you are probably running a marathon, not a sprint! Be gentle with yourself. Sweeten and Kreis both suggest that you lower your expectations of yourself, and decide what is really a priority.

9. Have fun with your children! Missing the parent who is absent does not have to mean that you cannot do fun activities while he or she is gone.

10. Everyone in the family needs to be patient and gentle with themselves and others during the postdeployment period. Often this is even harder than the separation.

Don't expect that things will be the same as before the deployment. Everyone has grown and changed. Spend time together, take it slowly, keep the kids' routine, and don't try to make up for lost time. Expect that children may act out. All of this is normal (American Red Cross). It is important to be patient and allow several months for everyone to readjust and to renegotiate family roles and responsibilities.

Seeking Professional Help

If you are the caretaker and become very anxious or depressed, find that you are not coping well, or feel like you are about to explode and take it out on the children, it is important to seek help. It is also important to seek help for the kids if problems persist longer than two or three weeks. Most bases have chaplains, support groups, and counseling centers. In military communities there are usually counselors who will accept your insurance. If you are not sure where to go, you can ask for a referral from your family doctor, chaplain, or the school counselor at your child's school.

If you are the returning parent and you find that you are experiencing a great deal of irritability, nightmares, flashbacks, jumpiness, feeling "numbed out," or distancing yourself from your family, these may be signs of posttraumatic stress disorder. It is important for you to seek help before it affects your family.

SOURCES

American Red Cross. "Military Members and Families." http://www.redcross.org/services/afes/0,1082,0_321_,00.html (accessed September 26, 2006).

Kreis, D. M. "Deployment Stress." http://www.sgtmoms.com/user/bkl/bkl_user_display.asp?action=display_object&ObjectID=19617 (accessed September 26, 2006).

Macias, Leigh (school counselor, Abrams Elementary School, Ft. Carson, CO). Discussion with the author, February 6, 2003.

Medway, Dr. Frederic (professor of psychology, University of South Carolina). Discussion with the author, February 12, 2003.

Military Advantage, Inc. "Your Children and Separation." http://www.military.com/Content/MoreContent1?file=Deployment_Family_Children (accessed October 12, 2006).

Pincus, Simon H., Robert House, Joseph Christenson, and Lawrence Adler. "The Emotional Cycle of Deployment: A Military Family Perspective." *U.S. Army Medical Department Journal* (April–June 2001).

"Schools Help Military Kids Deal with Parents' Absence." *Colorado Springs Gazette*, January 26, 2003.

Sweeten, Angela (military spouse, Pocassat, MA). Discussion with the author, February 15, 2003.

i miss you!

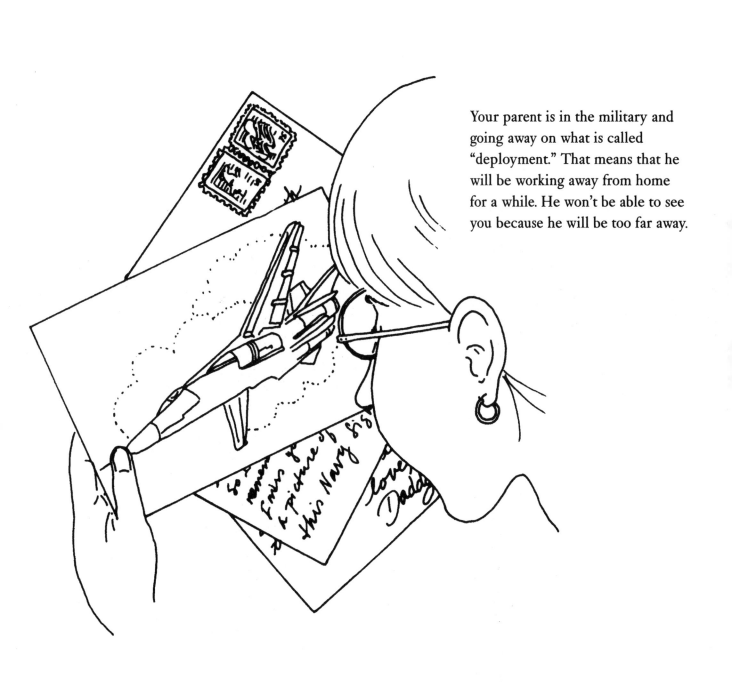

Your parent is in the military and going away on what is called "deployment." That means that he will be working away from home for a while. He won't be able to see you because he will be too far away.

It is important to remember that your parent
doesn't want to leave you.
She loves you very much,
and will come back as soon as she can.

Sometimes he can tell you when he will be back, but sometimes he doesn't know.

Can you draw a picture
of your parent who is
on deployment?

Sometimes parents go to another country on deployment.

You can ask your parent to show you on a map or globe where she will be going. Then you can learn something about that country, what they eat there, what kids do for fun, and how to say "hello" and "good-bye" in their language.

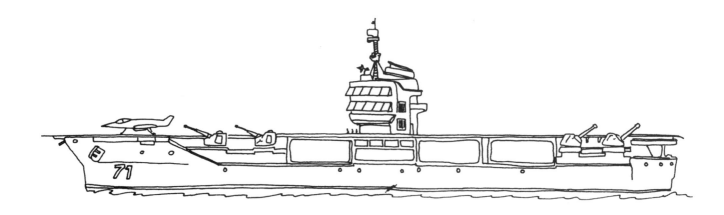

Sometimes it is a secret where your parent is going.
Then he may not be able to tell you, or he may not know.

Kids often ask, "Why do you have to leave?" Your parent is going to help other people and you can be very proud of him for that. It's like you are sharing your dad or mom with people who really need his or her help, and you can be proud of yourself for that.

Sometimes kids who know their parent is leaving soon have worries and questions like:

1. Do you know when you will be coming home?

2. How often can we e-mail or talk on the phone?

3. Who will take care of me? (There will always be a grown-up to take care of you, but you want to know who it will be.)

4. What will your job be like while you're gone?

Do you have any questions that you want to ask?

Kids may worry about whether their parent will be safe. Remember, your parent is well trained for the job he or she does. Lots of people have done this job before and come home safe and sound. But it's OK to talk about your worries and ask questions.

You may have other worries. It is OK to talk about these worries with a grown-up so he or she can help you feel better. But it doesn't help to worry a lot about things that may never happen. You can have fun and let the grown-ups do the worrying.

If it is your brother, sister, stepparent, aunt, uncle, or cousin who is away on deployment, you might also miss him or her a lot or be worried.

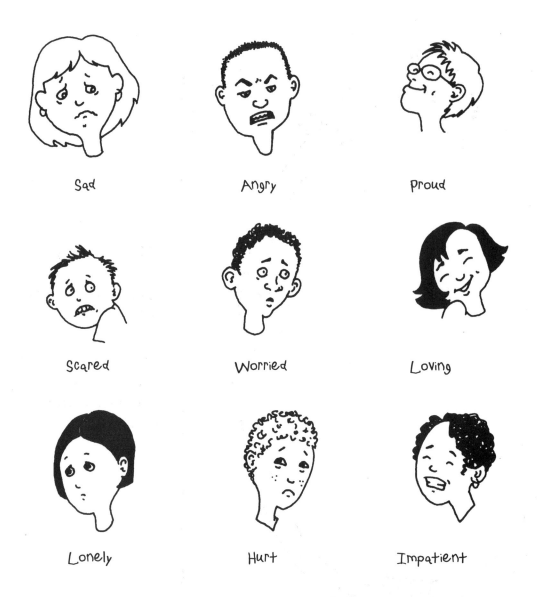

Sad

Angry

Proud

Scared

Worried

Loving

Lonely

Hurt

Impatient

Kids have lots of feelings while their dad or mom or another family member is away.
Do you ever feel like this?

Kids sometimes worry about having these feelings, but lots of kids feel this way.

Whatever you feel is OK. Draw a picture about what you are feeling today.

Sometimes kids are mixed up
or have a lot of different
feelings at once.
We call that feeling "confused."

Sometimes kids think it is their fault that their parent had to go away. It's important to remember that it is not your fault. You didn't cause it. Your parent went away because it is his job.

The parent or other grown-up who is staying home with you may be very tired and sad because she also misses your parent who is gone. Because she is trying to do everything that the absent parent usually does, she may get tired more often and may not have the energy she had when your parent was home.

It's OK to ask for what you need and if she can't do it, maybe she can help you find someone who can.

For example, kids sometimes miss wrestling and tickling with Daddy. Maybe your uncle or grandpa or a friend can do this.

It is also important to remember that it is not your job to take care of the grown-up who is staying at home with you. It is her job to take care of you. Your job is to go to school and play and have fun.

It helps to remember that you are not alone. Lots of kids have a parent or other relative on deployment.

There are many adults who care about you. These caring adults may include your parents, grandparents, aunts and uncles, school counselor, chaplain, teachers, babysitters, neighbors, and the parents of your friends.

There are things kids can do to help themselves feel better while a parent is gone.

For one thing, you can talk about your feelings with your parent who is home with you or with another caring grown-up.
Who are your favorite people to talk to?
Draw a picture of them here.

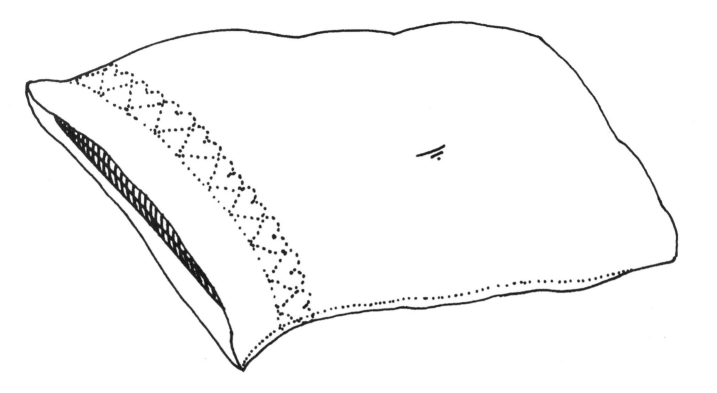

If you are feeling angry, you can punch something soft, like a pillow,
or you can go outside and kick a ball,
or just jump up and down to get some of the mad feelings out.

If you are feeling sad,
you can talk about it,
or sometimes it helps to
just cry for a while.
It's OK to cry—crying helps
all of us deal with sad feelings.

You can draw pictures
about your family
or your feelings.
Drawing pictures can
really help with feelings
that bother kids.
What would you like
to draw here?

Sometimes kids visit a therapist or counselor, where they talk, play, and draw pictures about the things that bother them. Counselors know how to help kids handle all the feelings they have.

If you have a pet, it can also help to cuddle and play with it. If you don't, maybe you have a friend who would let you cuddle with their pet.

Here are some other things that other kids have tried that help them feel better when they are feeling sad: send letters, pictures you draw, "care packages," your school papers, and pictures of things you are doing at home to the parent who is away. If you want to, sit down at night and write or draw about the important things that happened that day, and then send these.

Talk on the phone with and
e-mail the parent who is away
whenever you can.

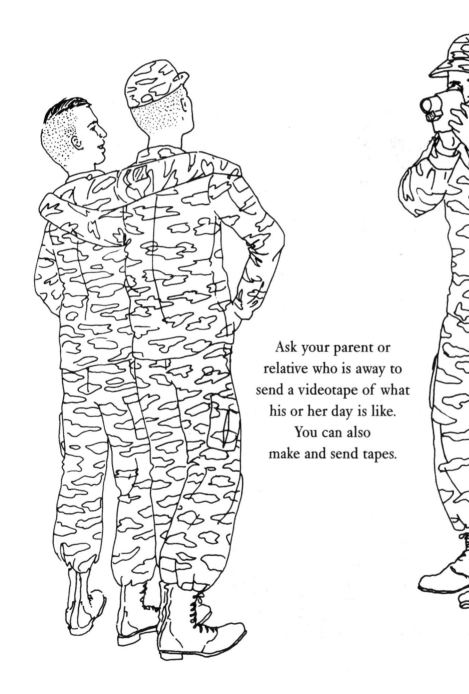

Ask your parent or
relative who is away to
send a videotape of what
his or her day is like.
You can also
make and send tapes.

Ask your parent who is about to leave
to make an audiotape or a videotape
of him reading stories or singing to you.

X out the days your parent has been gone on a calendar.
If you know when she is coming back, have a "halfway party" to celebrate halfway through the deployment.

Ask your parents or
another caring grown-up
to get you your own dog tags.
Put your parent's or
family member's name
on them so that
you can wear them
close to your heart.

Ask your parent who is leaving for a T-shirt he has worn
so that you can sleep with it.

Make a "paper chain" by decorating and adding one link each day of the deployment. Then you can use the chain to decorate the house for his homecoming.

Decorate a box
and use it to keep pictures
and special things
your parent or relative
who is gone has given to you.
When you are feeling sad,
you can look through the box.

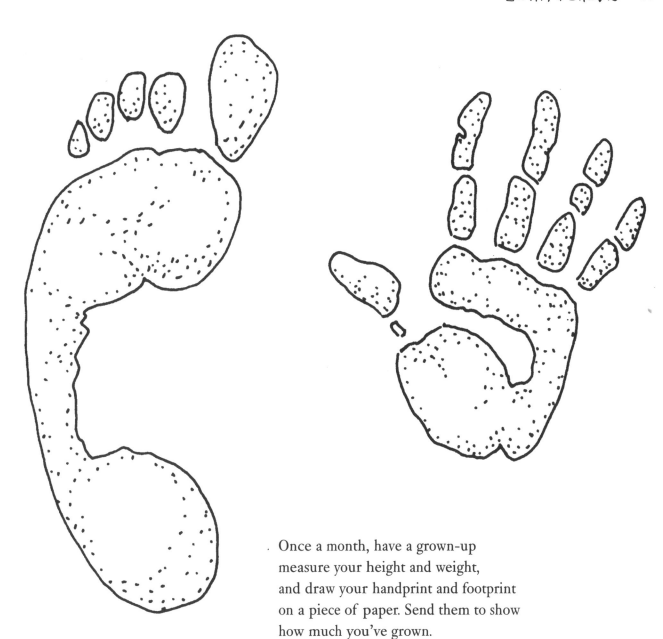

Once a month, have a grown-up
measure your height and weight,
and draw your handprint and footprint
on a piece of paper. Send them to show
how much you've grown.

Having a parent go away on deployment can be hard, no doubt about it. But you can make things easier for yourself. Just remember:

1. Your parent loves you very much and will come back as soon as he can.

2. You can be very proud of your parent or family member, and proud of yourself for sharing with people who need help.

3. It's OK to have any feelings you have about the deployment.

4. You are not alone. Lots of kids go through this, and lots of grown-ups care about you.

5. There are many things you can do to feel better.

And Tom would most certainly have been crushed beneath the creature, had he not – at that very instant – found that in his hand he already had a broken spray of the red berries. And as the monster toppled over onto him, he popped a berry into his mouth and bit it.

Once again the world began to spin around him. The clashing dinosaurs, the forest, the bubbling mud swamp, the fiery sky – all whirled around him in a crescendo of noise and then . . . suddenly! . . . There he was back in his own garden. The Joneses' washing was still on the line. There was his house, and there was his father coming down the garden path towards him looking none too pleased.

'Dad!' yelled Tom. 'You'll never guess what's just happened!'

Tom's father looked at the wrecked woodshed, and the dug-up vegetable patch and then he looked at his prize roses scattered all over the garden. Then he looked at Tom:

'No, my lad,' he said, 'I don't suppose I can. But I'll tell you this . . . It had better be a *very* good story!'

*   *   *

NOTE: If you're wondering why the magical tree with the bright red berries has never been heard of again, well the Stegosaurus landed on it and smashed it, and I'm afraid it was the only one of its kind.

Oh! What happened to the Stegosaurus? Well, I'm happy to be able to tell you that it actually won its fight against the Tyrannosaurus Rex. It was, in fact, the only time a Stegosaurus ever beat a Tyrannosaur. This is mainly due to the fact that this particular Tyrannosaur suddenly got a terrible feeling of *déjà-vu* and had to run off and find its mummy for reassurance (because it was only a young Tyrannosaurus Rex after all). So the Stegosaurus went on to become the father of six healthy young Stegosauruses or Stegosauri, and Jurassic Tail-Thrashing Champion of what is now Surbiton!

NICOBOBINUS AND THE DOGE OF VENICE

THIS IS THE STORY of the most extraordinary child who ever stuck his tongue out at the Prime Minister. His name was Nicobobinus [*Nick-Oh-Bob-In-Us*]. He lived a long time ago, in a city called Venice, and he could do anything.

Of course, not everybody knew he could do anything. In fact only his best friend, Rosie, knew he could, and nobody took any notice of anything Rosie said, because she was always having wild ideas anyway.

One day, for example, Rosie said to Nicobobinus: 'Let's put a rabbit down the Doge's trousers!'

'Don't be silly,' said Nicobobinus. 'The Doge doesn't wear trousers.'

'Yes he does,' said Rosie. '*And* we ought to boil his hat up and give it to the pigeons.'

'Anyway, who *is* the Doge?' asked Nicobobinus.

'How d'you know he doesn't wear trousers if you don't know who he is?' exclaimed Rosie (not unreasonably in my opinion).

Nicobobinus peered across the water and muttered: 'He doesn't live in the Doge's palace, does he?'

'Gosh!' said Rosie. 'I've never been fishing with a real genius before.'

'But he's the most important man in Venice!' exclaimed Nicobobinus.

'They've got universities for people like you, you know,' said Rosie, and she yanked a small carp out of the canal.

'What have you got against him?' asked Nicobobinus, as he watched her pulling out the hook with a well-practised twist.

'He's just extended his palace,' said Rosie, looking at her fish. It was about nine inches long.

'So?' said Nicobobinus, wondering why *he* never caught anything longer than his nose – which wasn't particularly long anyway.

'Well, he extended it all over my granny's house. That's what!' said Rosie.

'And now your poor old gran hasn't got anywhere to live?' asked Nicobobinus sympathetically.

'Oh yes she has! She's living with us, and I can't stand it!' replied Rosie.

Nicobobinus pretended, for a moment, that *he* had a bite. Then he said: 'But how will putting a rabbit down the Doge's trousers help?'

'It won't,' said Rosie. 'But it'll make me feel a lot better. Come on!'

'You don't really mean it?' gasped Nicobobinus.

'No,' said Rosie. 'We haven't got a rabbit – so it'll have to be a fish.'

'But that's our supper!' said Nicobobinus. 'And anyway, they've got guards and sentries and dogs all over the Doge's palace. We'd never get in.'

Rosie looked Nicobobinus straight in the eyes and said: 'Nicobobinus! It's *fun!*'

Some time later, when they were hiding under some nets on one of the little fishing boats that ferried people from the Giudecca to St Mark's Square, when the weather was too bad for fishing, Nicobobinus was still less certain.

'My granny says that where her kitchen used to be, they've built this fancy balcony,' Rosie was whispering, 'and she reckons any thief could climb in by day or night.'

'They drown thieves in the Grand Canal at midnight,' groaned Nicobobinus.

'They'll never catch us,' Rosie reassured him.

'Who's that under my nets?' shouted a voice.

'Leg it!' yelled Rosie, and she and Nicobobinus jumped overboard!

'Lucky we'd reached the shore!' panted Nicobobinus as the two sprinted across St Mark's Square.

'Hey! You two!' yelled the fisherman and gave chase.

Some time later, as Nicobobinus was standing on Rosie's shoulders pulling himself onto the balcony of the Doge's palace, he was even less certain.

'Have you got the fish?' hissed Rosie, as he pulled her up after him.

Nicobobinus could feel it wriggling inside his jerkin.

'No,' he replied. 'It was so unhappy I set it free. It said it didn't want to get caught by the Doge's guards in the company of two completely out-of-their-basket idiots like . . .'

'Look!' said Rosie. 'Do you see where we are?'

Nicobobinus peered into the room with Rosie and caught his breath. It was a magnificent room, with lacquered gold furniture and elegant paintings on the wall. But that wasn't what caught the attention of Rosie and Nicobobinus.

'Do you see?' exclaimed Rosie.

'Toys!' breathed Nicobobinus.

'We're in the nursery!' said Rosie, and she was. She had just climbed in.

Back at home Nicobobinus had just one toy. His uncle had made it for him, and, now he came to think about it, it was more of a plank than a toy. It had four wooden wheels, but the main part of it was definitely a plank. Rosie thought about her two toys, back in the little bare room where she slept with her sisters and her mother and her father and now her granny. One was moth-eaten (that was the doll that had been handed down from sister to sister) and the other was broken (that was a jug that she used to pretend was a crock of gold). But the Doge's children had: hoops, spinning tops, hobby horses, dolls' houses, dolls, toy furniture, masks, windmills, stilts (of various heights), rattles, building blocks, boxes, balls and a swing.

'There's only one thing,' whispered Rosie.

'What's that?' asked Nicobobinus as he picked up one of the hoops.

'The Doge hasn't got any children,' said Rosie, but before she could say anything else, one of them walked in through the door.

'Hasn't he?' said Nicobobinus.

'Well I didn't think he had,' said Rosie.

During this last exchange, the little girl who had just walked in through the door had turned pale, turned on her heel, and finally turned into a human cannonball, that streaked off back the way it had come.

'Quick!' cried Rosie. 'She'll give the alarm!'

And before Nicobobinus could stop her, Rosie was off in pursuit. So Nicobobinus followed . . . What else could he do?

Well, they hadn't got more than half-way across the adjoining room, when they both noticed it was rather full of people.

'Hi, everyone!' yelled Nicobobinus, because he couldn't think of anything else to say.

'That's torn it!' muttered Rosie. And on they dashed into the next chamber.

The Doge, who had been one of the people the room was full of, sat up in bed and said: 'Who are *they?*'

'I'll have them executed straightaway,' said the Prime Minister.

'No, no! *Apprehend* them,' said the Doge.

'At once,' said the Chief of the Guards.

'My clothes!' said the Doge, and sixteen people rushed forward with sixteen different bits of the Doge's clothing. Getting out of bed for the Most Important Person In Venice in 1545 was a lot more elaborate than it is for you or me . . . at least, it's more elaborate than the way I get up – I don't really know about you.

Anyway, by this time, Nicobobinus and Rosie had bolted through six more rooms, down a flight of stairs and locked themselves in a cupboard.

'Phew!' said Rosie. 'Sorry about this.'

'That's all right,' said Nicobobinus.

'Please don't hurt me,' said a third voice. Nicobobinus and Rosie looked at each other in astonishment (although, as it was pitch-dark in the cupboard, neither of them realized they did).

'Who's that?' asked Nicobobinus.

'I'm not allowed to play with other children,' said the voice. 'My nurse says they might hurt me or kidnap me.'

'Don't be daft!' exclaimed Rosie. 'Children don't kidnap other children.'

'Don't they?' said the other occupant of the cupboard.

'No. And *we're* not going to hurt you,' said Nicobobinus.

'Then why are you here?'

'A lark,' said Rosie.

'What's that?' asked the girl.

'You know . . .' said Nicobobinus, 'fun.'

'Fun?' said the little girl. 'What's that?'

'Oh dear,' muttered Rosie.

'Stick with us and you'll see,' said Nicobobinus.

'All right,' said the girl. 'My name's Beatrice.'

But before either Nicobobinus or Rosie could tell Beatrice their names, there was a thundering as dozens of people went storming and clattering past the cupboard shouting things like: 'There they are!' and 'No! That's not them!' and 'Ow! Take that spear out of my ear!' and 'Quick! This way!' and 'Look in there!' and 'Help me! I've fallen over!' and so on.

When they'd all finally gone and it was quiet again, Nicobobinus, Rosie and their new friend stuck their heads out of the cupboard. The coast was clear, except for the guard who had fallen over.

'Give me a hand would you?' he asked. 'This armour's so heavy that once you fall over it's very difficult to get back on your feet again.'

'Doesn't that make it rather hard to fight in?' said Nicobobinus as they helped him to stand upright.

'Hopeless,' admitted the guard. 'But it *is* very expensive. Now, have you seen two children go past here?'

'Yes,' said Beatrice. 'They went that way!'

'Thanks!' said the guard and ran off as fast as his expensive armour would allow him. He'd got round the corner before he must have realized he'd made a mistake, for there was a crash and a muffled curse, as he tried to stop and turn, but fell over again instead.

'Come on!' yelled Rosie.

'Is this fun?' asked Beatrice, as they ran up another staircase and onto a long balcony and looked out over a narrow street.

'Are you enjoying it?' asked Nicobobinus.

'So-so,' said Beatrice.

'Then it's probably fun,' said Nicobobinus.

'Oh! Stop wittering, you two!' exclaimed Rosie. 'And help me down off here!' Rosie was already climbing over the balustrade and hanging from the balcony.

'That's too far a drop!' exclaimed Beatrice.

'You wait!' grinned Nicobobinus. 'We've done this before.' He whipped his belt off, and before you could say 'Venice and chips!' Rosie was clinging to the end, and being lowered down into the street.

'Oo-er!' said Beatrice.

'Come on!' called Rosie.

'Are you sure this is fun?' whispered Beatrice.

'Well it beats enjoying yourself!' shouted Nicobobinus, as several guards suddenly appeared at the far end of the balcony.

'Hurry!' he said, and thrust the end of the belt into her hand.

'There they are!' shouted one of the guards. And without giving another thought, Beatrice followed Rosie down into the street.

'Nicobobinus!' yelled Rosie. 'How are *you* going to get down?'

'I'll be OK!' yelled Nicobobinus, although his main thought, as he ducked through a window, was actually 'Cripes!'

'I thought you'd done this before?' said Beatrice as she and Rosie legged it down the street.

'Well . . . maybe not from quite such a high balcony,' admitted Rosie, and they disappeared round the corner.

Nicobobinus meanwhile had made a discovery. He had discovered that the window that looked out onto the long balcony that looked over the Calle de San Marco was the window of the office of the Prime Minister. He also made a second discovery: it was office hours. The Prime Minister was sitting on a sort of throne, holding an audience with several rather scruffy individuals who looked scared out of their wits.

'. . . and then take their heads off,' the Prime Minister was saying, as Nicobobinus backed in through the window and landed in front of him.

'Ah!' smiled the Prime Minister, signalling to his guards, 'another customer.'

Some time later, Nicobobinus found himself chained and shackled and being dragged into the Grand Audience Chamber of the

Doge of Venice himself. It was a particularly magnificent room, and nowadays people come from all over the world to gaze up at the ornate ceiling and stare at the fine furnishings, while a guide talks too quickly in a language they can't understand and tells them about all the boring and pompous men and women with famous names that have come and gone through the doors of that famous place. But one story they never tell (and I don't know why) is the story I'm telling you now.

At that particular moment, however, the one thing Nicobobinus was *not* interested in was the magnificent decor of the Grand Audience Chamber. His one and only concern was how to get out again as quickly as possible (which, come to think of it, is probably what most of today's tourists are thinking too!).

'Bring the boy here,' yawned the Doge (who was actually wishing he was back in bed).

'We could start by simply cutting his feet off, and then move on up to his knees . . .' the Prime Minister was whispering in the Doge's ear as Nicobobinus was thrown onto the floor in front of them.

All eyes were upon him, and an excited buzz went around the Audience Chamber. The Doge looked at him for several moments and then said: 'What are your demands?'

Nicobobinus thought he hadn't heard right, so he said: 'I beg your pardon, Your Highness?'

'Where is she?' shrieked the Prime Minister, and suddenly everyone in the room was muttering and shouting the same thing.

'Silence!' commanded the Doge. Then he turned to Nicobobinus once more and said: 'You have kidnapped my daughter. I will give you what you want, providing you return her at once – unharmed.'

Nicobobinus was just about to say: 'No! I *haven't* kidnapped your daughter', but he didn't. Instead, he looked around at all the heavy, brooding faces, the wine-soaked noses and the sunken eyes of all the important, pompous folk of Venice, and he said: 'I want one thing.'

'Yes?' said the Doge.

'And it isn't for me,' went on Nicobobinus.

'It's for your master,' assumed the Doge.

'No,' replied Nicobobinus, 'it's for your daughter.' A gasp went up around the room. 'It's something you must give Beatrice.'

The Doge couldn't speak for a moment, but eventually he managed to say:

'And what is it?'

'Fun,' said Nicobobinus.

'Fun?' said the Doge.

'Fun?' said all the pompous and important people of Venice.

'Fun!' said another voice, and there was Beatrice, the Doge's daughter, standing at the entrance to the Grand Audience Chamber, holding Rosie's hand. 'We've been having fun!'

Well, to cut a long story short, the Prime Minister still wanted to chop off Nicobobinus's and Rosie's heads and drown them in the Grand Canal at midnight, until the Lord Chief Advocate pointed out (after consulting various medical authorities) that you can't drown someone once you've cut their head off.

'Then just drown them like the rats they are!' exclaimed the Prime Minister.

'But they're only children,' said the Doge's mother.

'That's beside the point!' screamed the Prime Minister. 'It's the *principle* that matters! If you don't drown them, soon you'll have all the riff-raff of Venice climbing into the palace and making demands!'

But the Doge had fallen asleep, and his mother ordered that Beatrice should decide what was to become of Nicobobinus and Rosie. Beatrice said they had to come and play with her every Monday. And so that was that.

Later that evening, as the Doge was getting into bed, and all the assistants were gone, he said to his wife: 'You know, my dear, a most extraordinary thing . . . Just now . . . Do you know what I found in my trousers?'

At about the same time, Nicobobinus and Rosie were sitting on Nicobobinus's doorstep laughing and laughing as Nicobobinus described how he had managed to slip the wriggling fish past the Doge's belt and into his trousers while the Doge's mother was kissing him goodnight.

'But one thing puzzles me,' said Rosie. 'When did you stick your tongue out at the Prime Minister?'

'I didn't,' replied Nicobobinus. 'That happened in a totally different adventure.'

'Was it the one where we set off to find the Land of Dragons?' asked Rosie.

'Ah!' said Nicobobinus. '*That* would be telling . . . '

AUG   2008